You Can Trust The Conservatives (To Be Conservatives)

This is my extended book review of the book "You Can Trust the Communists (to be Communists)" by Dr. Fred Schwarz.

Definition of hypocrisy
plural
hypocrisies
- **1:** a feigning to be what one is not or to believe what one does not: behavior that contradicts what one claims to believe or feel; especially: the false assumption of an appearance of virtue or religion.

Definition of communist
- **1:** an adherent or advocate of communism

- **2:** capitalized: communard

- **3a** capitalized: a member of a Communist party or movement **b** ofte n capitalized: an adherent or advocate of a Communist government, party, or movement.

Definition of conservative
- **1:** preservative

- **2a:** of or relating to a philosophy of conservatism **b:**capitalized**:** of or constituting a political party professing the principles of conservatism: such as (1):of or constituting a party of the United Kingdom advocating support of established institutions (2):progressive conservative

- **3a:** tending or disposed to maintain existing views, conditions, or institutions: traditional conservative policies **b:** marked by moderation or caution a conservative estimate **c:** marked by or relating to traditional norms of taste, elegance, style, or manners a conservative suit, a conservative architectural style.

To regard oneself as conservative is to exercise conformity. As most adults understand, a degree of conformity is essential to the ability to assimilate into human societies. These human societies have evolved economic systems that channel progressive productivity for the overall good of that society.

Societal economy as a cultural machine was not especially scrutinized as such before the 1929 market crash and subsequent Great Depression. Ancient economies were agrarian and singular as well as commercial, before evolving further into communal efforts. The industrial revolution has evolved national citizens from subsistence farmers into mercenary workers, toiling together towards territorial, empirical autocracies.

Yet these human citizens working toward the grand abstract ideal of brighter futures have few civil rights as working citizens. Based upon the premise that no man owes another a living, pensions for retired workers are not guaranteed as rights in capitalist economies. As the US led the world in this industrial revolution which has so profoundly shaped the course of civilization in such a massive experiment, it formulates policies along the way during the passage of time by political remedies, such as the New Deal and Social Security systems.

As an economic system, capitalism must follow a linear direction through history. There was once in America's recent past a time where conservative capitalists considered the communist ideology so adverse of a threat to their well-being that they published a mountain of propaganda to counter what they expected to be a war of wills, with the possession of Earth and its inhabitants the spoils.

Upon analysis, with the benefit of hindsight, it has been learned by the majority of sentient minds that the specter of communism and its accompanying evils were greatly exaggerated and overrated. Nevertheless, paranoia remains among those occupying the lunatic fringe.

In a perfect world under perfect circumstances, anyone interested in themselves would desire to be conservative.

One observed trait of the modern conservative is assumed uniform conformity, another is opposition to non-conformity. To label perceived threats to such conformity under the blanket condemnation of any pejorative epithet (e.g. communist) is to engage puerile and pusillanimous antipathy.

It may have been the situation that America needed a nemesis after defeating the Axis threat in 1945, and found it in the political/economic system that enthralled part of the Old World. Communism. Its old wartime ally. As a dedicated foe to another long-established economic system, capitalism. To some people, to be non-capitalistic is to be communistic, even if currency pursuit is not a factor in the lives of others.

This contest between dueling economic/political systems, capitalism and communism, consumed the energies and lives of billions of humans closing out the twentieth century, while spilling into the twenty-first. What was accomplished?

Any perfect politics, perfect economic system, perfect religion or perfection in any other endeavor achieved would gain only adherents, and never critics. The amount of problems each attempt at perfection achieved develops indicates how far from actual perfection such attempts prove to be.

What is a capitalist, a communist, a socialist? I'm a worker. If I voice opposition to a capitalist, am I automatically a communist? If I oppose communism, will capitalism save me? If capitalism can serve to enrich the merchant class, the celebrity class, the professional sports athlete class, the executive class, the landlord class, the corporate class, the investor class, the aristocratic class, the noble class, the academic class, the managerial class, the political class... then why not the working industrial peasant class?

Dr. Schwarz makes the claim that class war is a contrivance of the communist party. Communists are not guilty of wealth disparity and wage stagnation. One may be led to wonder what "class war" is anyway, since both Marx and Dr. Schwarz wrote about it.

I don't know what class war is other than what I've personally experienced as a worker. I certainly have learned what class discrimination, class segregation, and class restriction are. The caste system is alive and well in the land where all men are created equal.

Because any good conservative would quickly emphasize that all people are not created equal. And this is a point as yet not clarified: what levels are equality and inequality met and set?

The class war is and always was. It was realized internationally during the organized labor movement during the 19th and 20th centuries, as a sibling to the Industrial Revolution. And it was certainly manifested as a cause in other international events, such as the Russian Revolution of 1917.

Doctor Frederick Charles Schwarz MD was an actual medical physician, born on January 15, 1913 and who died January 24, 2009, according to his biography. Presumably his death was not caused by Communists or their sympathizers. That he was a doctor, as well as a writer and polemicist against what he termed Marxism/Leninism, causes one to wonder why he perceived such a nebulous threat to be so jeopardizing to his manner of living.

In his Wikipedia entry, he is considered an expert on Marxist/Leninist doctrine. W hen we as modern readers delve further into the subject, we discover the words made from people's names to distinguish historical national policies: Stalinism, Maoism, Marxism, Leninism, Trotskyism, et.al. This would indicate cults of personality, which are not labeled thusly in American political arenas as Nixonism, Eisenhowerism, Kennedyism, and/or Johnsonism. Joseph McCarthy found a way to turn his social campaign into his name suffixed, and all to the detriment of intell ectual freedom, as time has shown.

What was Doctor Schwarz not? Definitely not a communist. Not a Nazi, although his family originated from the same nation Herr Adolf did. Might have definitely been a conservative, and certainly a capitalist, since his books sold and made him some money.

Probably was never a blue-collar worker. Never spent time in unemployment lines filling forms and pouring sweat waiting or talking to indifferent people for the privilege of a job interview to labor at a position which means excessive exertion for dismal remuneration. Never had to endure harsh environments nor dangerous conditions in order to get a physical task completed. Never spent time as a farmer where only agrarian subsistence meant the difference between eating and hunger. Never spent time homeless. No excessive time on his feet, or serving endless rude customers, or soliciting strangers for the bare necessities. Never came home from a day's work exhausted, stinking with sweat, stiff with fatigue. Never hurt on a job. It's easy to speculate how many people never had to endure many harsh hardships.

It's easy to surmise that he never spent much time as a soldier on the front lines getting shot at by hostile forces for questionable motives. Nor could there have been much time in ditches digging with shovels, nor carrying heavy items between points A and B, nor many years spending daily hours at a factory trying to maintain a pace of productivity someone else set, nor wearing a costume masquerading as a uniform for an enterprise that pays minimum pittance without benefits for the sake of another person's profit. Never scrubbed a floor nor cleaned a room in anxious anticipation of a critical inspection. It may be imagined by those who do these things that those who don't do similar things have indeed been somehow blessed by a society that has not acknowledged them for their own selfless efforts.

Can he have ever been wrung with indecision or compromised identity, plagued by the stress of not knowing where in life to turn, or which was the most beneficial courses to embark upon?

Communists obfuscated with the visage of supporting workers, exampled in their infrequent appellations of terming themselves "Workers Parties." One might be inclined to retort that capitalists view workers as little more than mere chattel and pawns, animated props or disposable commodities. The truest disenfranchised subsets of civilization might prove to be the common manual worker, upon analysis. How is any manual worker allowed any decision-making leverage in cond ucting daily business, other than by offering his presence and doing his duty?

No one in their right minds presumes to assert that workers are not necessary evils: one cannot run a country using only princes and princesses. The boding question for contemporary conservatives and capitalists to resolve is how much further can they wring from an over-wrought productive class? How many more instances of self-interest in the name of the collective corporation shall the individual sacrifice for?

Dr. Schwarz uses subtle hyperbole and negative analogy to theme his message. The cover of his book, "You Can Trust the Communists (to be Communists)" has this shakily drawn picture of three adult males behind a post with barbed wire, presumably to represent political prisoners. On the second page, he's invoking the threat of child molestation, cancer, and bank robbery to parallel disreputable behavior with his declared opposition to world-wide Communist philosophy. This is a contrived intention to set a negative tone.

He wrote that it was important for Americans to understand the philosophy of communism as he understood it, to know the enemy. It's easy to glean that he understood the parts he wanted to acknowledge. It may be wondered whether radical communists and radical capitalist conservatives differ greatly with certain aspects of herd mentality exampled by mindless ceremonial ritual and gang obedience. As in military parades and formalized pomp. Such is encouraged for the sake of tradition, among other excuses.

Dr. Schwarz makes the most peculiar assertion on page 25:

"Contrary to the expectations of Marx, the ownership of American industry is constantly enlarging. There are now nearly as many stock holders in the United States as there are members of organized labor. It is quite conceivable that in a short period, the number of stockholders will exceed union membership. This renders the whole argument of the 'class war' ridiculous. Nothing does such damage to the principles of Marxism as the development of worker ownership in American industry."

According to Dr. Schwarz, not only is there not a class war, but it's better to have greater amounts of Wall Street investors than it is to have productive union workers. Let's analyze such claims closely.

Does Wall Street itself know how many investors it has? Probably not. How can any entity know any constantly changing amount? How many workers are there, union and non-union? What are the battles in any class war? And what do these workers end up owning? Homes, or debt?

We can research labor demographics. From 1964 to 2014, there were drastic and widespread reductions in workers participating in organized labor, from 30% of the entire force to around 10%; coinciding with the widening wealth gaps that have bee n duly noted.

The question of class war may start to be addressed by scrutinizing the conservative capitalist's opinion of organized labor. When is that opinion ever favorable? The worn adage of impoverished citizens pulling themselves up from the depths of poverty in order to participate in the swelling collective of happy societies is diminished by such weapons in class war such as reduced fringe benefits, lack of enforceable pro-worker laws and regulations, unenforced immigration laws allowing migrants to take domestic jobs, H-1B visas promoted over job training for those eligible, and many other intentionally engineered obstacles.

The criticism of organized labor is invariably accurate. Too many ways during the past decades the unions have compromised to the benefit of the corporation. In the past, there were far too many abuses committed, and by those who seemed well-intended but may have been just as well agents provocateur. Pensions looted, and not only placed in questionable investments, but such perfidies only given tepid legal investigations. How far did the collaboration of crony corruption finally extend? During the Second World War, the U.S. Government collaborated with organized crime as well as Russian communism. How much do all three infiltrate each other?

Dr. Fred Schwarz criticized socialism. Professor Albert Einstein supported socialism. The criticism was thus made that as a physics professor, Einstein didn't understand economics. How much more so could Dr. Schwarz have misunderstood a field he wasn't educated in, yet taught in? Is it not peculiar that Dr.Schwarz never published any memorable treatise in his field of expertise? And again it may be queried why the world's best economists can't solve the world's most pernicious economic problems.

What normal-minded human would prefer to do hard, dangerous, and poorly-paid work; such as being in the military? Only those who originate from the most dire of circumstances, generally. Why else the sacrifice, for pitiable gain? What could motivate another to endure privations that don't recompense accordingly and fairly, other than necessity?

Military members can not be represented by union, and aren't even regarded as a normal class of employees. The hard truth is they're understood to be government property under Article 15 of the UCMJ. For lower echelon rank-and-file, the military service obligation contract becomes similar to time served under a penal sentence. For the offense of penury. But not life sentences except by choice.

The penury is socially engineered to keep its convicts penurious. To put it in other words that need more emphasis, *the poor are intentionally left poor and kept p oor.* Capitalism as an economic system oft abuses those it uses, and debases more th an it benefits. It's a policy of exclusionary tactics in order to provide its own type of particular communal welfare: supporting leaders in preferable career positions of authority who have proven themselves by their very physiques incapable and unfit to conduct physically-demanding labor.

To criticize capitalism is not to embrace communism or denounce capitalism, despite what the hysterical may infer. It may prove the best hybrid system for operation will be a combination of systems. Such as what presently exists.

Again, the question: is there class war? Dr. Schwarz denied there was class war in capitalism, and it can be proven that such denial is contrary to reality rather easily. Most economically lower class of demographic subject to rules and regulation imposed by faceless bureaucracy have proven their subservience by their very servility, as would have helots of old. The differences between these classes are distinct, and separated by chasms of requirements for academic accreditation. Without the necessary credentials, applying for jobs out of one's field proves to be an exercise in futility.

On page 14 Dr. Schwarz publishes a curious repetition. "Stalin assumed power when the Communists were a beleaguered garrison and he brought them to the verge of world conquest." Followed shortly thereafter in the same paragraph: "Stalin brought Communism to the very verge of world conquest." The redundancy is telling. Barring editorial error, it may be that this specific example of propaganda polemics is the familiar mantra of prevarication, embellishment, and repetition. The ability to persuade of any speaker is directly proportional with the listener's ability to critically analyze. Without critical analysis, many assertions made are allowed as *prima facie* evidence, and innocent until proven guilty.

Has not the time of history proven the political/economic system of communism to be ethnic/region specific in its governance? Does not its own durability establish its own form of continuity, and thereby success; albeit limited by its own scope?

Dr. Schwarz cited instances and anecdotes of atrocities presumably committed in the name of communism by its adherents, and it is to be universally acknowledged that atrocities are atrocious. He frequently claimed in his writings to know how communists think and thought, and their sinister ways to infiltrate then influence America's culture. Incredible claims are alleged, such as "... a majority of the students in the world today are attracted to communism." (page 18)

To honestly think that is true requires a great stretch of imagination.

He goes on by elaborating how communists are recruited, molded, indoctrinated, then set to their tasks of moral and ethical infiltrating corruption to an international cadre of a youthful generation. They always do it for the kids.

On page 24 one opportunity of capitalism mentioned and available for the modern working American human is the offer of consumer credit, lauded as an outstanding benefit. As that it is, it's also beyond debate a debt obligation. At many periods in time as civilizations evolved, defaulting of debt obligations became regarded to be criminal offenses.

Is capitalism being operated intelligently when it binds a nation's peasants to life-long debt obligation for mere shelter? To whose benefit will the productive class be despoiled? To what extent? How much honor will the successful, prosperous nation gain by glorifying the exalted while debasing the lowly? We have been raised all our lives with our minds indoctrinated by the cooperative collaboration of Wall Street with Madison Avenue through mass publishing current events by means of a state-approved media. For the glorification of the citizen elective? For a nameless, ambiguous grand cause?

How may capitalism or any other system of human grading patterns establish an inherent human worth of individuals without utilizing a stringent method of testing and intelligently planning its societies to accommodate that masses of worthy citizen attain beneficial niches? Using this present chaotic system of trial and error, coupled with successive series of accidents, is a definitively haphazard way to procreate generations of human sapiens.

It's all in the numbers, to the nascent man entering the workforce to sell his health and strength and intellect to a vast job market. The numbers of currency units earned, and accruing life's necessities and wants from the amounts of such numbers. Seeking a career course, which may or may not prove finally fulfilling.

Is it wrong to wonder if capitalism grades and places all people in sequential, incremental steps, with at least one hundred levels? Thereby defeating any pretense of equality alleged? May we gauge the worth of every human by their capacity to earn currency in an industrial, capitalist society? Is the successful human's legacy the amount of wealth aggregated over the course of a life? Will the imperative of sustaining existence contribute from all enabled bodies capable to the communally civilized global village?

Shall we let this define our purpose for existing? Each guided by their own spontaneous impulse?

It's more coherent to be timorous of commuters than communists. Four generations of motorized vehicular transportation have crafted an evolved human who can, with experience, drive in traffic daily with the skill of the most proficient adept. It's done internationally, by billions of people. Who each dread even close proximity with other folks driving, in order to avoid collisions. How many of them are communists, intent upon subverting the democratic republics of capitalism? How may such competitive commuting not bring out unsocial revulsion to our fellow humans? A form of transportation-induced misanthropy.

Commuting teaches us this inalienable fact: keep the other person as far away from you and yours as possible. In vehicles at high rates of speed, this is always sound advice. How may this reticence at human contact not translate over into social interactions when not commuting? When do the traits of being unsocial degra de to becoming anti-social?

Also on page 24 Dr. Schwarz dares to promote the optimistic prognostication of motorboats as commonly owned as cars. Curiously omitting the existence of classes of menial workers who dare not even dream of such extravagant luxuries. What type of atypical peasant may indulge in conspicuous consumption using disposable and discretionary income that exceeds their needs? Will there be enough time from one's career to waste time so imprudently; instead of gaining additional academic accreditation, pursuits of self-development, devotion to applying one's off hours to overtime in order to help the corporate company, to devote effort and hours to community service?

Are there not slums, ghettos, apartment projects, and trailer parks even in the world's most prosperous nation that house the lowest of human wretches, outcasts, and misfits? Capitalism must attempt at explaining failure, as well as its own successes, in order to evolve.

The attempts of the elite capitalist rulers of the working peasant class against the right to protest probably extends to the beginnings of civilization, but surely manifested itself during the decade of the 1960s, where scurrilous sideline slander alleged that communists had subverted and infiltrated the peace protests against the war in Vietnam. In my personal possession I have the most quaint religious tract by a "Bro Maze" that dates itself quite well. Entitled "What's Behind the Race Trouble in the South?" In this tract, the premise is made that the NAACP was a communist front organization, led by some ambiguously identified "master minds in New York." No evidence of communist influence is offered other than an imperfect transcription of a speech made by a Roosevelt Williams at a "secret" NAACP meeting in December of 1954. Then the subject of the message digresses sharply away from the title and intent of the publication.

The text inveighs against teenage immorality. Amusing enough, until the section that tentatively castigates AMERICA'S TEEN-AGE IDOL. A new singer, by the name of Elvis Presley. The tract accurately reports Ed Sullivan's $50,000 offer for three shows, calling the amount of money "fantastic." Mentioning the film "Love Me Tender" dates the tract to around or after November of 1956.

The "great joke" that no one ever understood at that time was how Mr. Presley would only fourteen years later collaborate with conservative Richard Nixon to condemn drug abuse and anti-American influences during the sixties, then die from irony self-inflicted by 1977. Conservatives select their cultural enemies on the basis of their own particular narrowed frame of reference, despite what else may prove to be mitigating factors.

It's easy to propose the notion that times were different back then, and the stalwart enemies to America's puritanical ideals of ethics and morality are no longer the same as they were. Yet to the new generation of self-entitled and critical judges of proper culture, the commies remain the same, even if they're not quite as visible.

Mentioning visibility is to mention physical appearance. And what other human beings on Earth are so discriminating, so passionate, so incredibly judgmental about the looks of others than modern American conservatives? Appearances and impressions left by those appearances seem to be of primary importance to those to whom looking good is more essential than doing good.

We were certainly warned. My memory remembers the lesson of social studies class that presented drawings of the same young male, drawn three different ways. One was drawn to present him and ugly and unsightly, one drawn to cause him to appear average, and one to cause him to look handsome and intelligent. Then the insightful inquiry began: which of the three would you hire? Which would you rather speak to, or be friends with? Which of the three would you trust? Which will be your enemy? Which of the three is going to get further in life than the other two? Which one would you avoid? Which was smarter, which less intelligent?

The point can never be emphasized enough: how personal appearance dictates identity, then thereby destiny. One does not expect their doctor to look like a construction worker. Professions are occupied by human people that relate to those professions by means of their own physical identity.

Wouldn't this be considered a massive failing on the part of any broad social experiment at civilization that yielded to base human nature from such superficial criteria? To be so shallow that one could think integrity would be wrought from shaved apes and their standardized visages? To think that young attractive females hold more inherent worth than unattractive male workers is to idealize questionable moral values and a pandering to unrestrained procreative instinct. Yet such vast discrimination is prevalent. Supermodels don't beg on street corners. Assignment of value based upon visual appearance.

And so the study seems to fly off into oblivion. One perpetually unanswerable query would be is the inner person reflected outwardly in an accurate fashion? Is it not true that so many of us find in life that we are slaves to our bodies and genetic inheritances, with these randomly-selected cages of flesh our sole means of ambulatory transportation?

Capitalism and conservatism are a married couple that often walk hand-in-hand. One would expect the ones with all the money and power to want to keep their money and power, despite how it may have be derived. This is natural human nature. To be stingy, and disinclined to share. Children exhibit these traits naturally. Conservatives will want you to appear conservative too, to prove solidarity with their established ideals, carried over from prior generations.

So the hyperbolic warnings continue, to nearly feverish pitch. Page 33: "What will be your attitude when you and your family face destruction because of your me mbership in the historically rejected Capitalist class? As the wide-bore revolver with the soft-nosed bullet is placed at the nape of your neck to shatter your Capitalistically conditioned reflexes into a bloody oblivion..." Fear used as a method of persuasion. The entire treatise is one long warning. The graphic description is, of course, quite a lurid farce.

American culture has proven to be at war with itself for a long time, but much more so during the decade of the 1960s, after the long, perhaps serene period of 1946-1960. Elvis bothered grandmothers and other puritans. Then the Beatles and Dylan came to corrupt the fragile little minds of America's youth with psychedelic drugs, long hair on males, and alternative ways of thinking. Decades later, rigid conservative doctrine will dictate that long hair on a man is indeed a shame, and such rules will influence sanctimonious objectification in segregating social assignment of such endemic misfits as those populating countercultures. This cultural means of martial grooming is a remnant of the animosity against anti-war radical protesters in the 1960s by pro-war conservative factions.

Full beards may be tolerated. Trimmed beards, mustaches, shaved heads, shaved faces. All acceptable codes of grooming for proper conservative status quo life, as physical conformity in appearance is essential when out in public and assimilating into cultural castes. Just don't wear long hair. Your bosses will tell you what clothes to wear and how to "professionally" appear, you don't tell them.

Compare the news reporters and anchors of every television show. All fitting strict grooming guidelines. To a flaccid public receptive to being guided into the conformity of popular status quo. Even up to and beyond such peculiar social phenomenons as the "red scares" of the 1950s, which undoubtedly partly prompted the writing of Dr. Schwarz's book.

Proper conservative doctrine has also long held that the ingestion of cannabis and its derivatives was also forbidden, upon flimsy and manufactured evidence which always proved quite specious at best and absurd at worst. This condemnation of a natural herbal remedy has proven contentious by conservative cultural swings, when utilized against disadvantaged sectors of the population using draconian punitive measures. Prohibitions and screenings by means of testing have been implemented at places of employment, but not universally applied to areas in dire need of labor. Their attempts at seeking perfection in an imperfect world have left quite telling results. This is class discrimination in action. But it's not a war if the attacked don't fight back. Ergo, at-will doctrine in employment.

Hypocrisy is finely embodied in any policy or law which declaims cannabis use for loss of intellect while failing to criticize the brain damage such popular occupations as professional football inflict in the form of concussions upon its participants. Then for corporations to use such excuses later as a sifting process during employment qualifications and legal systems as punitive retribution is proof enough, from the view of the lowest rung of social strata, to be retaliatory.

Proper conservative doctrine indignantly rebukes, and rebukes often. It is quite vocal in keeping the policies, laws, rules, and people in power where they are; while simultaneously acting as an agent against any and all change it feels improper or not fitting for distinguished folk. Even by using such sales tactics as fear, shame, and patriotism.

Dr. Schwarz closes his second chapter with more flight of his active fantasies, imagining how communists are indoctrinated against all the progressive things

America has produced for the sake of civilization; thus to be eschewed and scorned by the enlightened, atheistic, ungrateful, intellectual straw-man student of historical sociology for the sake of another type of attempted utopia.

Chapter three begins with the tumultuous beginnings of Russian communism and the subsequent purges, progroms, and show trials such a violent foreign revolution brought about. When viewed from historical hindsight, foreign attempts at installing communism as a political government seems to be a revolutionary doctrine to replaced ingrained despotism with more despotism. That appeals to peasants, instead of intellectuals. What kind of intellectual approves of and supports institutionally applied, despotic communism? Only ones that profit from such power structures.

Administrative management of the Russian communistic political structures are elaborated further, with suspiciously intricate detail.

The study of history teaches the student that nations come and go, empires rise and fall; revolts and revolutions, civil wars and civil insurrections happen when ruling powers abuse those they rule. One may nitpick human atrocities and cruelties *ad infinitum*. It's the mercies that get less attention. The fine line between benevolent rule and enforced despotism can develop many degrees. Humanity has historically proven that it can endure generations of hostile, tyrannical reign, from many instances. Revolt when it does occur is rather infrequent, even if yet so consistently applied through history. So, to fear the change of political revolution is demonstrably futile, unless one has a deep vested interest in conserving that which is in place.

What motive to sell the fear of imminent political revolution, that occupied the hearts and minds of American propagandists for so many decades? What gain was produced, sowing trepidation among a nation of voting successors to frontier pioneers? Were these constant caveats the paranoid scenarios of established business classes?

What else could they have been? To have been so vehement, and so errant?

More author repetition follows in pages 48-49. Page 48: "All power resides in the Communist Party." Page 49: "All power is in the Communist Party." Repeating it often. Almost as a chant.

Dr. Schwarz closes chapter three with a measure of historic truth, that the "curse of Communism" was used as an instrument of dictatorship, tyranny, and genocide. All this is factual, enacted by generations that preceded us living now. In what name of what god, political, and/or economic systems were all other unnamed monstrosities committed, over the vast expanse of time past? If communism as a movement failed, was it because of erudite warnings by well-intentioned authors, or was it because of its own inherent weaknesses? And if it failed because it was doomed to do so, could that ultimate demise not have been foreseen, making dire warnings against it unnecessary? It's always laudable intent: to oppose tyranny and oppression, no matter what it calls itself.

Personally, I have met as many communists in my life as I've met Manicheans. Exactly none. No one expects that every Chinese peasant in China is a communist, so to count their immense population as a *de facto* membership is inaccurate. The same may be said of Russia, and its peasantry. It's easier to claim more American citizens have memberships in the one of two factions in America's capitalist party. Understanding, of course, that a two-party political system is only one party better than a totalitarian regime of one political party.

After all these complete descriptions of how the typical communist is recruited then molded, chapter four details how the communist convert works. Page 54 details that "...the Communists came to power in Russia and China by the reverse policy of the distribution of land, by making everybody a little Capitalist." Curious statement, since that is precisely what capitalism does. But in America, the peasant has to buy the land, post-Homestead Act. He then related an anecdote of how he examples how communists stay in power, through threat of lethal force against revolt. Precisely the way capitalism in the United States prevents violent *cou p d'etat.* Such assertion is incredibly easy to prove: try starting a violent revolt of your own, and see how long you last against the mightiest state forces in history.

It's a selling point for the success of capitalism, how a certain percentage of the population can realize an amount of disposable income above and beyond mere subsistence. The revolution becomes superfluous to a contented population amenable to tolerating a certain degree of official political corruption through means of undue monetary influence, as long as the masses of the peasantry aren't suffering excessive hardships.

Page 54 continues with "The Communists go to the working man and promise him higher wages, shorter working hours, and better conditions generally." As workers, workers have seen capitalists and their politicians not promise, but deliver low and stagnant wages, longer working hours, and many other worse conditions generally; until the development of the twentieth century organized labor movement. It's a biased perspective, to point out the faults and flaws of one system while never admitting to abuses rife in the other.

Communism pre-dates capitalism in human history as an economic system, but capitalism evolved from a barter system of exchange. True and unadulterated communism has never been exercised in practice by any modern civilized government, only totalitarianism, and it may prove to be an impracticable economic system when managing mass populations. We may presume that capitalism is adulterated; forced into social paradigms by regulatory legislation. Such was the reasoning behind efforts against corporate monopolies, usury, resource hoarding, and other abuses.

Dr. Schwarz accuses the fervent communist of practicing deception through the guise of delivered promises. In short, a real sneaky way to win folks to your cause is to vow certain social reforms, the way any politician of a democratic republic would do. He next warns against "communist front groups," that provide an easy excuse for the average concerned citizen to identify and malign as possible suspects for cultural infiltration and subversion. Thus, many civic groups which exist now are made targets of indolent slander and libel.

The anticipated vitriol against the conservative's most virulent enemy, the dreaded liberal, begins at page 60. "Most of these liberals are to be found in the ivory cloisters of colleges and universities, frequently occupying professorial chairs, and usually characterized by a pseudo-intellectual outlook." This is clearly an *ad hominem* assault on intellectuals *en masse*. "Pseudo-intellectual" is a convenient, sloppy slur used by those who scorn how logic proves superior to reaching reasonable conclusions than faith and innuendo do. Such a criticism is immature, and always better left unsaid. If we want people to act and be smarter than they really are, you should never condemn them for trying to exercise greater intelligence than what they get confronted with. As humankind tries so hard century after century to purge from his memories so much mistaken knowledge accumulated by ancestors over time passed.

Capitalism is scarcely under any type of credible threat. This is proven, with communist China finding itself forced to adopt it to a controlled extent. 100 years after the Russian Revolution, do the Russians now practice actual communism?Albeit democracy needn't be included in the bargain. But those who won't be convinced by persuasion will be deceived by guile, in the minds of the zealous. Would Jesus have been a capitalist? Or would his Kingdom of God yet to come be a democratic republic, or a socially conservative laissez-faire police state, full of ivory cloisters? Are heavenly politics as well imagined as the other aspects of afterlives?

It may be considered hypocrisy when the modern conservative mind-set reacts more indignantly to looters during natural disasters than the price-gougers for emergency necessities. When those in control display admiration for the select and s corn for the common, they reward those who deserve it least and punish those who deserve it least.

These university professors are told the attitude they take, to be against censorship, dictatorship, brutality; yet tolerant enough to allow communist conspirators to infest. Dr. Schwarz claims that these people contend "...no restraint or restriction of any kind should be applied to an individual because he has availed himself of the Fifth Amendment." Page 60.

It may prove preferable to err on the side of individual rights, but courts may not rule in that manner. The applicability of coerced, non-criminal testimony against oneself shall be as protected as criminal testimony, per *Garrity v. New Jersey,* 1967 He expounds further upon constitutional law on page 61, writing: "The Fifth Amen dment refers merely to imprisonment and legal penalty. Any attempt to project it beyond that realm is not intellectualism or liberalism, but stupidity."

This places his favor directly to the state in most matters of individual self-incrimination. As do so many protestations from those who consider themselves conservatives, rather than for the individual liberties of the free citizen. This is a distinct difference in types of political doctrine. Is freedom a higher priority than na tional security?

The first question should begin: how insecure is the nation, that it must devote so many and so much to achieve security? An easy question no one has ever displayed enough intelligence to address.

Rights are to be universally applied, not conditionally applied. Rosa Parks taught us that. To restrict the right to remain silent to criminal proceedings alone is not to proclaim it to be inapplicable anywhere else a citizen may feel the inclination to not speak.

The next sub-chapter of chapter four is entitled "The Liberal's Dilemma." This diatribe perhaps more finely identifies the practitioners of doctrine most offensive to typical American social conservatives.

Dr. Schwarz's "liberal dilemma" is written out as a exemplar from a contrived, imagined circumstance in the manner of a parable. He invokes admittedly "ridiculous situations" to explain errors "pseudo-liberals" neglect to understand in how toxic communist ideology is. His error is that they're not being pseudo if they're being as consistently untrustworthy as he suspects they are. They're being genuine. Sometimes it would seem that liberals are considered greater enemies by conservatives to conservative ideas of republic than socialists, communists, fascists, anarchists, and monarchists combined. Such divisive vitriol may be simple venting, yet exposes deep chasms of contention.

To simplify, he could have lumped the communists with the fascists, the pacifists, the imperialists, the liberals, the socialists, and anyone else of dissimilar opinions as tyrants, and proclaimed himself anti-tyrannical. John Wilkes Boothe proclaimed the same. Defense of the status quo is as safe as praising a god that already has all the power.

On page 63 begins the section THE BIRTH OF A FRONT, perhaps one of the main motives behind the book's origin. In it it is written: " An organization which had the announced purpose of weakening America militarily so that the Communist conquest would be easier would rally few supporters." Page 64 continues: "Therefore there must be an announced objective which will accomplish the same purpose, but which will present itself in a totally different guise. This is the basis of the array of unholy peace movements spawned by Communism."

How can the words unholy and peace be combined with sanity? Its antonyms would be holy war. Such as the Crusades were, and Islamic *jihad*.

Hindsight tells us now of how bizarre any prediction is that claims the United States military can be weakened by much of anything on the planet beyond its capacity to weaken itself. The most incredibly complex and expensive destructive force in all of human history, bureaucratically administrated through layers of levels. Here we find ourselves once again confronted with obvious anomaly, over the course of nearly sixty years.

Dr. Schwarz beseeches readers to beware the communist sympathizer, the fellow traveler, the pseudo-liberal, the unwitting members of front organizations disguised as some other social camouflage, the duped patriotic businessman; all possible tools for the intrigues of communist front organizations. Beware involuntary involvement, as a pox to the liberty of America. America becomes an ideal now as holy as God, intolerant of sin or sedition. A discerning god that will tolerate only the acceptable.

The American conservative sees the ceremonies called Pledge of Allegiance and National Anthem as patriotic quasi-holiness, not to be maligned nor disrespected by non-participation. If you engage in any ritual that requires mindless obedience, then you're participating in something that approximates mob mentality rather than analytical cognition. It's never mentioned that such obeisances are formalities exhibited in the praise of freedom, and to be coerced into acknowledging such is self-defeating, as well as aberrant. To be forced into any type of obedience is to be cheated of freedom. Any who do not participate in the ancient traditions of ceremony are to be suspect of nationalistic apostasy.

Page 67 details the history of the Russian Revolution of 1917 and the rise of Vladimir Lenin, entitled TECHNIQUES FOR SEIZING POWER. On page 68 he differentiates between Marx and Lenin, by the established history of Lenin's propensity to violence. Which causes one to wonder why the need to combine the philosophies of the two.

The first plot to overthrow the established state was identified as infiltration of ex ecutive positions in labor unions. Now, it's easy to stand back and make any wild guess about anything. But if one was to speak directly to any of the many union officials throughout the country or world, how many of them would claim to be a communist in any shape or form, even knowing there would be no repercussion? As a communist plot, this plan had to be doomed to failure from its inception. Workers are mercenaries trying to survive in a world where everything costs something. American workers are disinclined to organized communism, as a rule. Even Che Guevara was unable to get peasants to toil for scrip. Labor strikes are not therefore, communist plots against capitalist economy; they're a means of securing more humane conditions for those who toil for a living.

Dr, Schwarz goes into greater detail of how the industrial strike somehow morphs into a political strike, then a revolutionary strike. Then further, an exposition of communist involvement in Australian labor unions during the late forties and early fifties. He admits freely that the so-called revolutionary strike has not yet brought the communists any success (page 74), then laces his history with inferences not citing other sources how strikes were coordinated for rehearsals for revolutionary power seizures. He freely admits to democracy working in Australia, by the communist party candidates for public office consistently being allowed to run for public office, yet remaining unelectable.

Dr. Schwarz uses the excuse of national emergency in Australia to break a coal strike that occurred in 1949. The leader of one local being communist, the other local that didn't honor the strike anti-communist. Without knowing specifics, who can say with what intent strikes were called and not honored by others? Maybe there were communist influences then, but are there now?

So of all the labor unions there were back then, this other one used as an example that is called International Longshore and Warehouse Workers' Union was indeed expelled from the Congress of Industrial Organizations for communist influence in 1950. In 2013 the ILWU disaffiliated from the national organization. Such is evolution. How much communist influence is practiced now? By leadership, by membership? Or is it practiced at all?

Page 83: "The formation of all transport unions into one association such as that being considered at present under the leadership of (Jimmy) Hoffa and (Harry) Bridges carries potentials of great danger. A mass transport strike could so paralyze this country that starvation and death would be rampant in every part." (Parentheses mine.)

Is this so? If indeed it was possible, it never did happen. What did happen was that Harry Bridges retired in 1977, and Mr. Hoffa disappeared in 1975.

"The mechanism outlined by the Communists is still in operation. It is not completely out of date. When workers can be compelled to join organizations, contribute their money, and obey the leadership imposed by a small group. When th at money can be used for political purposes by a constant propaganda campaign by the press, radio, and television so that the public may be influenced to elect legislators under obligation to the union leadership, the very foundation of republican, democratic government is in danger. When government becomes irreversible, dictatorship is at the door."

What really happened was that the federal government itself got incredibly entangled with bureaucracy, and the labor union influence shrank over the decades. As did the earning power of the average worker as the economy outsourced manufacturing and wealth disparity increased.

In 1965, U.S. CEOs in major companies earned 24 times more than a typical worker. By 2007 it was 275 times that of the typical worker. In other words, in 2007 a CEO earned more in one workday (there are 260 in a year) than the typical worker earned all year.

"The American Promise is that if we go to school, work hard, and become a productive and faithful employee, we can then expect to support a family, raise and educate our children, enjoy a healthy and fulfilling life and retire with dignity. We weren't supposed to have to win the lottery, or be a corporate executive to enjoy the American dream. That was the vision of middle class Americans, who once modeled the image of what it was to be an American. The middle class is disappearing in direct proportion to the demise of the American union movement. After World War II, nearly 30 percent of our work force belonged to unions. Today, barely half that are organized. Wages of $8 per hour are common. For most of these workers there is no health insurance or retirement plans. The result? Taxpayers across the United States are making up for what employers should be paying with public assistance programs. That's corporate welfare. Why are wages so low? Because that's the easiest way to increase profitability. The result? Today, the wealthiest one percent own as much of our nation as ninety percent of the rest of us. Corporate CEO's can earn 500 times the wages paid their workers." Quote from a labor union website. We were warned about the excesses of organized communism, and about disorganized capitalism. But conservatives defend how capitalism needs to abuse as well as use its lowest common denominators.

Chapter six on page 84 recites the history of three nations taken over by communists: Russia, China, and Czechoslovakia. The latter of which no longer retains tangibility as a sovereign country. Time has yet to tell if Russia has renounced communism, although is seems to have certainly retained the exercise of oligarchical totalitarianism. Oligarchy is a disease of crony capitalism, not communism.

Has there ever been a serious academic study to investigate whether communism as a political and economic system has been beneficial for China as a whole? What were the results for Cuba, where the brutal communism there overthrew a previous brutal regime? Have the oriental nations of Vietnam and Laos lapsed, prospered, or simply stayed stationary?

Speculation of what could have been is idle, in the wake of what has been.

Chapter seven is subtitled The Dictatorship of the Proletariat. Only zealous partisans seem to use such words as proletariat and bourgeoisie. Especially in colloquial conversation. The dynamic of worker/management relations remains the same, despite what titles executive power choose to use. There is a rule declared in quotation by Vladimir Lenin, that " ...the rule, unrestricted by law and based on force, of the proletariat over the bourgeoisie, a rule enjoying the sympathy and support of the laboring and exploited masses." Called by Dr. Schwarz as "the dictatorship of the proletariat."

How the "proletariat" dictates anything at all has yet to be explained. Dr. Shchwarz interprets Lenin's words to mean " ...the rule, based on force and unrestri cted by law, of the Communist Party over everybody else." Although this is not what was said.

So the tactics for revolution and planning against counter-revolution are detailed. "Children are set to spy on their parents, wives on their husbands, employees on employers, pastors on their congregations, parishioners on their pastors." The government-declared drug war of the following decades in the United States mimicked similar means of encouraging citizens to inform authorities of suspected crimes.

Dr. Schwarz ends this chapter writing that only "knowledge can enable" his audience to resist such insidious tactics of dialectic and subversion. Quoting J. Edgar Hoover who called such agents "Masters of Deceit." Irony notwithstanding.

Chapter eight outlines the ALLIES OF COMMUNISM. Using an amusing and obviously fictional story of a rabbi, Irish cop, and a priest to illustrate how belief makes differing interpretations of reality in people. Then presents five instances of evidence for the "impending Communist conquest" in his reality interpretation.

 • *Numerical evidence*. This is printed as "five children in school learning in detail the godless doctrines of Communism, for every one child in any school anywhere learning anything about Christ. These facts are fearful to contemplate, but they are inescapably true." Those facts seem a little too precise as well. Why would one mass opiate be preferable over another? Does Jesus approve of capitalism? How does the notion of a supernatural messiah play into national economies?

 • *Military evidence*. Dr. Schwarz relates applicable anecdotes, then proffers p redictions on the future by "Big Business electronic computers" of the estimated balance in military power becoming favorable to Russia over the US. The estimated year given for Russia to become stronger than the US in military might was 1965. In the amount of time since then, Russia and the US had fruitlessly invaded Afghanistan; the US additionally launching wars twice in Iraq and once in Vietnam, forays and sorties; with Russia in the Crimea and Ukraine too, and all to achieve what? *De facto* and proxy intervention? Soldiers killed, leaders assassinated, governments overthrown and new ones established. Military might itself becomes moot when both large nations are convinced they both can destroy the other. Now the issue becomes convincing smaller countries not to destroy themselves.

 • *Educational evidence*. He claims that Russia graduates three times the amount of engineers and scientists. Don't know if that was true then or true now without doing the necessary research, but America still makes interesting scientific discoveries to the present day. Dr. Schwarz makes a brilliant point about misplaced priorities in a personal anecdote he experienced how on his visit to a university he was introduced to an exceptional athletic student, but was unable to meet an exceptional science student. As it is, the US still lists impressive achievements in science and sports.

 • *Economic evidence*. The success of the communist economic system against the capitalist economic systems should be readily assessed using the economic evidence. "The Russian economy ranks as the twelfth largest by nominal GDP and sixth largest by purchasing power parity in 2015." Contrast the economy of the US: "... the world's largest economy by nominal GDP and second-largest economy by purchasing power parity." Quotes from Wikipedia. The preferable economy will prosper, if the economy which helps the greatest amount of people is preferred. All this is self-evident. What remains as not so sane is the amount of trepidation expressed by conservatives. Capitalism is the default mode for civilizations. To imagine that it could be supplanted with anything else is a nuance unfamiliar with reality. Even communism must acknowledge the laws of supply and demand. Page 109 says: "The Communists are doing a similar thing on a world scale. They can move into any American foreign market they consider desirable. They do not need to make a profit; their profit is in the chaos they create in the American economy, in the agents they infiltrate into the country through their trade." A rather vague comparison to capitalists as well, after the corporate globalization initiatives in the latter half of the twentieth century. Yet profit still seems to be made, things are still produced, and life goes on for all except for those rudely interrupted. Even fear-mongers need to earn. Fiat currency is still currency.

* *Communications evidence*. "The world is divided into three major areas: there is the Communist area, a great prison containing a billion slaves; there is what is known as the Free World consisting of America and her allies; and between these two, there is the uncommitted area of the world which numbers one billion people. These countries are the great battle ground between East and West. If the Communists secure them, they will have two billion and their superiority will be absolute. One hundred people are being reached with Communist lies for every one being reached with the Christian or democratic truth." So, how have the propaganda wars influenced *your* way of thinking? How much actual communist propaganda have any of us ever seen? Amid the mountain of capitalist, democratic, conservative republican propaganda that eternally derides the other propaganda? Mostly a war of words between those who war with words.

Page 114: "There are many things which may be said by way of criticism of America, but when all has been said, the fact remains that America is the magnet that draws to its shores people from all over the world. It is still the land of hope and promise, a vision living in the hearts and minds of millions." Undeniable, yet those seeking better lives are refugees. Millions immigrate, billions stay put. Refugees have been a part of human migration patterns long before there were nations. Page 115: "While America is being lulled to sleep with a false picture of friendship and talk about co-existence, the Communists are making devastating progress in many parts of the world. They are operating in all the Asian countries, in Africa and the Near East, and are looking forward to the time when Western Europe will be economically strangulated and defenseless; they are invading South and Central America by their infiltration of colleges and universities. When these countries have been taken, America, isolated, confused, and demoralized, will be offered the choice of surrender or annihilation. The Communists are certain that she will choose surrender." Imagine all this really happening. Not even in the most brazenly fictional movies do such contrived scenarios occur. The communists have proven that they're not numerous enough and organized enough to "take over," and America's not disorganized nor out-numbered enough to allow itself an overthrow. This type of amusing scare tactic proves itself so errant with hindsight's benefit.

On page 117 Dr. Schwarz admits he'd never been to Russia nor any other communist country. To dismiss this disadvantage, he compares his visits to America where certain things did and didn't happen over ten years he personally witnessed, such as racial discrimination, violent crime, and auto accidents. Because he didn't see these things happen in America, he hypothesizes for the sake of argument they didn't happen at all. Which is supposed to be the impression one gets when on a guided tour of a foreign country by those wishing to cast a favorable impression. The gist of which being, he infers that opinions are formed fr om only a superficial contact with cultural norms, and remain inflexible and permanent.

The eighth chapter concludes with the debated numbers of Baptist churches in Russia, and analogizing a football game with insidious communist obfuscation, by accusing the Great Foe of making pretenses of freedom while subtly inhibiting it.

Chapter nine is entitled BRAINWASHING. Some may believe that washing brains lead to clean minds. Brainwashing is another means of using ideology to over-explain persuasion. To explain the methods of brainwashing, Dr. Schwarz cites a story of Ivan Pavlov and his experiments with dogs and conditioned reflexive responses to trauma; then lists several torture techniques, including imposed physical exhaustion, confusion, chronic physical pain, and fear as tools in the brain-washers' arsenals. It may have assisted Dr. Schwarz to learn that Pavlov himself despised the Russian Soviet communists.

America itself has yet to clarify its own stance against using torture versus "enhanced interrogation techniques" against suspected malefactors. As in the lesser of two evils, are those who torture and brainwash less not as wicked than those who do it more? Or is it true that might makes right, and the ends justify the means?

Chapter ten is tedious indeed. Entitled THE DIFFICULT, DEVIOUS, AND DANGEROUS DIALECTIC this chapter is adroitly encapsulated by the author himself by his own definition of "dialectic materialism." He establishes that "Dialectic Materialism is the philosophy of Karl Marx that he formulated by taking the dialectic of Hegel, marrying it to the materialism of Feurbach, abstracting from it the concept of progress in terms of the conflict of contradictory, interacting forces called the Thesis and Antithesis culminating at a critical nodal point where one overthrows the other, giving rise to the Synthesis, applying it to the history of social development, and deriving therefrom an essentially revolutionary concept of social change." A better question would be what does any of this have anything to do with anything? Reality, matter in motion, philosophy, idealism, realists, materialists are disseminated in detail. Instead of the adage of the falling tree in the forest making sound, Dr. Schwarz uses wild waves against a shore. One might go as far as to wonder if the universe itself makes sight or sound to the deaf and blind. If only for the sake of the observer.

Dr. Schwarz does get around to pillorying "progressives" at page 150, ostensibly to be regarded as differentiated from liberals and student intellectuals. The last sentence of the page states "The Communists in labor unions always refer to themselves as the 'Militants' or the 'Progressives.'" Anyone who spends any time at all around any American blue-collar labor union hiring hall would be challenged to discover either progressives or communists disguised as progressives.

Dr. Schwarz concludes the section reporting on Premier Nikita Khrushchev and his tour of America in 1959, speculating upon his psychology and ulterior motives. The next section is spent detailing the nature of dialectic tactics to trick ordinary, common citizens. Claims are made that the good communist will support the Marxist ideals of marriage abolition and promotion of atheism, even by utilizing camouflage by practicing the opposite. Seems you can't even trust those with the best of intentions, since their intentions themselves may be concealed.

Page 156 "Genuine church leaders who were devoted to Christ were arrested, brainwashed, tried, and destroyed." Why destroy that which you've brainwashed? Unless he meant both as separate charges against specific, unnamed people. Once again, vague allegations and insinuations. Using a religious tactic called "moral maneuverability," that allows the fervent communist infiltrator access into any religion by adapting to the local culture's standards. Further space in the chapter details more complicating, over-analyzed, imagined plots and sub-plots to a grand conspiratorial web of intrigue.

Page 159 Dr. Schwarz once again enunciates the final goal of the communist movement by historical analysis: the class war is and remains the field of haves versus have-nots. To lack is to be deficient. Both sides want as much as they can wrest. For the future, Dr. Schwarz says that Karl Marx predicts a critical juncture where slow changes in dynamic industrial power structures turn into civil insurrections. The very nature of change changes. This double-talk serves to vilify certain identified social groups negatively, such as the "reformists" in page 159. Thus producing the evil of a new "synthesis," called socialism; and new social groups, called socialists. This becomes a part of the overall social transition Dr. Schwarz challenges what he claims the enthusiastic communist envisions. "If Capitalism MUST change into Socialism by a dialectic process, why MUST Socialism turn into Communism by a non-dialectical process?" Again, more thinking in absolutes.

It is claimed in the book that "when a baby is born, it immediately begins to wither, but the process of withering demands growth to maximum strength." This explanation of the natural life development stages conveniently ignores the maturation stages of organic life, and reveals itself to be quite unfamiliar with cellular degeneration. All this trouble to go through for the demise of all free peoples?

In chapter eleven, Dr. Schwarz claims to have testified before the House Un-American Activities Committee in 1956. He may have told them his opinion that was iterated on pages 174 and 175: "Each year the Communists appoint thousands of full-time Communist agents, primarily recruited from students who are motivated, dedicated, and thoroughly indoctrinated with Communism. They equip them with beautiful literature, and send them round the villages to deceive the peop le by offering them heaven on earth. We do not have thousands, but we have some hundreds who have a motive to sacrifice in the fight against Communism.

Communism is the enemy of their God, their Christ, and their freedom. Because of this, they are willing to go to their people and warn them of the dangers of Communism."

As should have been done with the boy who cried wolf, critical analysis is necessary to discern which dangers deserve the higher priorities. Of course, due vigilance need not be relaxed in the times of peace, instead of war.

Dr. Schwarz continues with some additional conclusions that sound suspiciously progressive themselves. Page 180 "The unity of a free society resides in its diversity." Page 177 "Communism should be taught in the schools but it should be taught with a moral directive." Page 175 "At present rates of progress, Communism will have conquered the world within a generation..." Page 181 "This liberty of conscience itself should direct the individual into unselfish service to fulfill his responsibility towards God and to the preservation of that liberty for all men."

Are we to never remember that all beings imbued with life shirk the fatal blow, and avoid pain instinctively? Even insects display these tendencies. What right do any of us assume when we take life from another living being? By what authority? So in the end, all any of us want is to gratify our most base desires, along with our most basic needs. Communists, capitalists, anarchists, nihilists, socialists, fundamentalists, humanists. All homo sapient.

He desired to conclude poignantly, as do many of us. Page 182: "Fundamentally, the problem is a moral and spiritual one. The foundations of freedom must be girded with a moral and spiritual revival. As free men humbly seek God and present their bodies minds, and hearts to their country and the cause of all mankind, we may well believe that tyranny shall not triumph and freedom shall not perish from the earth." Almost a parody of an Abraham Lincoln speech. Telling in some of its assumed concern for the sake of humanity's future. Rather a socialistic aspect of concern. Capitalism must need socialism, in order to profit from those it employs. Thus we discover that capitalism can never be extinguished nor seriously imperiled. Which discovery will never obviate the need to alarm for those who would warn of its impending demise.

"O Lord our God, help us to tear their soldiers to bloody shreds with our shells; help us to cover their smiling fields with the pale forms of their patriot dead; help us to drown the thunder of the guns with the shrieks of their wounded, writhing in pain; help us to lay waste their humble homes with a hurricane of fire; help us to wring the hearts of their unoffending widows with unavailing grief... for our sakes who adore Thee, Lord, blast their hopes, blight their lives, protract their bitter pilgrimage, make heavy their steps, water their way with their tears, stain the white snow with the blood of their wounded feet! We ask it, in the spirit of love, of Him Who is the Source of Love, and Who is the ever-faithful refuge and friend of all that are sore beset and seek His aid with humble and contrite hearts. Amen."

-Mark Twain

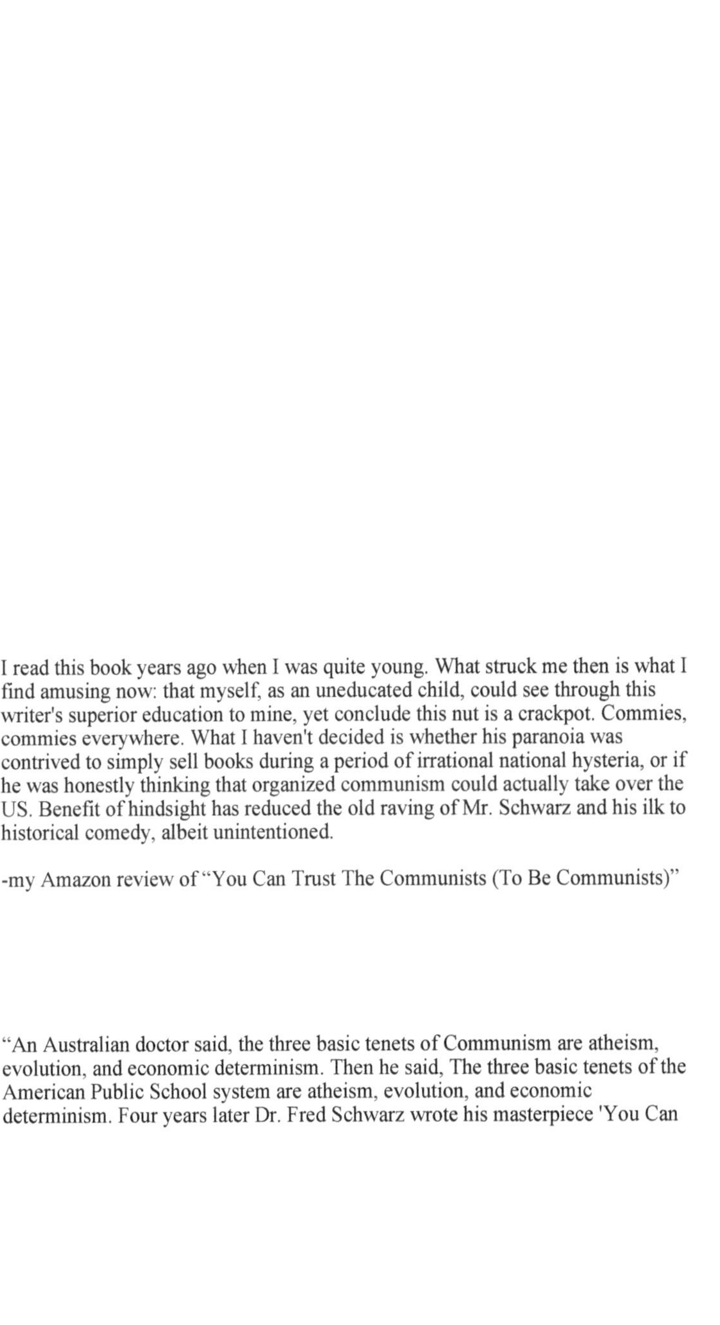

I read this book years ago when I was quite young. What struck me then is what I find amusing now: that myself, as an uneducated child, could see through this writer's superior education to mine, yet conclude this nut is a crackpot. Commies, commies everywhere. What I haven't decided is whether his paranoia was contrived to simply sell books during a period of irrational national hysteria, or if he was honestly thinking that organized communism could actually take over the US. Benefit of hindsight has reduced the old raving of Mr. Schwarz and his ilk to historical comedy, albeit unintentioned.

-my Amazon review of "You Can Trust The Communists (To Be Communists)"

"An Australian doctor said, the three basic tenets of Communism are atheism, evolution, and economic determinism. Then he said, The three basic tenets of the American Public School system are atheism, evolution, and economic determinism. Four years later Dr. Fred Schwarz wrote his masterpiece 'You Can

Trust the Communists (to Be Communists).' The republication of this book could not be more timely as America decides whether to follow its Christian forebearers or once again test the poisonous waters of Marx, Lenin, Mao, Castro, Alinsky, and their swarming collectivist agents and useful idiots in their relentless attempt to dethrone God and destroy Capitalism.

-Dr. Tim LaHaye review of "You Can Trust The Communists (To Be Communists)"

The term "useful idiots" should be regarded as self-referential to those who regurgitate convenient propaganda which sets with their particular world-view, whether such a view is even slightly accurate.

-me

So you think I'm a loser? Just because I have a stinking job that I hate, a family that doesn't respect me, a whole city that curses the day I was born? Well, that may mean loser to you, but let me tell you something. Every morning when I wake up, I know it's not going to get any better until I go back to sleep again. So I get up, have my watered-down Tang and still-frozen Pop Tart, get in my car with no upholstery, no gas, and six more payments to fight traffic just for the privilege of putting cheap shoes on the cloven hooves of people like you. I'll never play football like I thought I would. I'll never know the touch of a beautiful woman. And I'll never again know the joy of driving without a bag on my head. But I'm not a loser. 'Cause, despite it all, me and every other guy who'll never be what he wanted to be are still out there being what we don't want to be forty hours a week for life. And the fact that I haven't put a gun in my mouth, you pudding of a woman, makes me a winner.

-Al Bundy

We can trust the conservatives to tell us what it is we're doing wrong, whatever it is we're doing.